Tango On

Also by PJ Karr, Ph.D.

Catchin' the Sun and Moonbeams, Dad... Play, Laugh, Love
2013 Archway Publishing

40 Ways to Stretch Your Smileage
2011 Dorrance Publishers

AHA Epiphanies to Release the Spirit Within
2009 Dorrance Publishers

Tango On

Attitude = Altitude

PJ Karr, Ph.D.

Archway Publishing books may be ordered
through booksellers or by contacting:

Archway Publishing
1663 Liberty Drive
Bloomington, IN 47403
www.archwaypublishing.com
1-(888)-242-5904

ISBN: 978-1-4808-1161-4 (sc)
ISBN: 978-1-4808-1162-1 (e)

Library of Congress Control Number: 2014917561

Printed in the United States of America.

Archway Publishing rev. date: 10/15/2014

Flapper Gals and Glitz

Dedication

To those kindred and evolving spirits who...

want to live more fully in the "now"

want to enhance the opportune moments to "pause"

want to awaken their mind, body, and spirit

want to honor the amazing art of "becoming"

want to welcome the joy of playtime and laughter

Contents

Acknowledgments

MY FIRST CREATIVE NONFICTION BOOK WAS WRITTEN AFTER the academic surf and turf publications of thirty years. It was chock full of epiphanies that arrived after the infamous, midnight pumpkin and into the wee hours of the morning. Those "aha" moments deserve acknowledgment for their mystical, rejuvenating appearance and indelible imprints.

My adventuresome spirit catapulted. I went viral and wrote two more creative nonfiction books. In the interim, the local Planet Fitness wanted quotes from my first book, *AHA Epiphanies to Release the Spirit Within,* to appear in their foyer. "People will come into the foyer to our gym *and* be inspired." Grateful earthlings of all ages kept sharing, "I look forward to reading Dr. PJ's weekly aha's" and "I was so *inspired* by today's quote!" The alchemy began to happen! My dreamscape of another book with engaging epiphanies and photography emerged and blossomed.

I am grateful to be able to give kudos for the evolution of my "tango on" spirit. Throughout three decades, I had shared my early spirit, momentum, and motivational stories with my students, family, and friends. Now, the "tango on" spirit became a sensational fire in my belly.

Then, something else appeared. A "no coincidence"

moment arrived in the summer of 2014. My endearing friend of forty years refreshed my heart and soul. His amazing boldness and certainty with cancer treatments and our bona fide, heartfelt dialogues enlivened and revitalized my book endeavors (more than he envisioned or knew in his wildest dreams!). Thank you, JJM, for your witty soul, the "tango on" momentum, and the radiating, luminous light.

To my beloved Reiki master teacher, Angela, my cup runneth over with gratitude. You have been witness to my heartfelt writing endeavors. Sat Nam, my soul sister.

To my ingenious and impassioned readers—Liz, Marty, Gerry, and Steve—you possess an authenticity to attune, give, and receive. I am honored and humbled.

To Antonio, who embraces the 143 and our Isle of Capri, I remain full of joy. Thank you for the infinite "magic carpet" bliss which is destined to enhance my writing. Namaste.

To my eternal touchstones—Madre, JJ, and Patti—your unconditional love resonated during the earnest and significant stages of my writing. I am blessed with abundance.

Introduction

I WAS ALREADY WRITING, ALMOST FINISHED WITH MY BOOK, and suddenly, the mystique happened. Most writers will confess. We rarely know when, where, or why this phenomena occurs.

Voila! I knew the introduction for my book. It was no coincidence. The vibrant spirit of my Italia story, along with the exquisite persona of Federica, influenced and bolstered the pages in each chapter.

Our Trafalgar tour group had finally arrived at the Rome airport. Italy was no longer surreal. Jet lag reigned paramount, but our guardian angels (Federica and the hotel staff) magically found our suitcases and hotel rooms and even provided a festive, welcome dinner. Once aboard the bus for an early evening tour of Rome, an amazing feat in the jet lag mode, our group *really* became enchanted. Why?

One phrase: First-class, fiery Federica. She became our Queen Diva for the next ten days. Federica was a tall, striking woman who exuded a confident air and energy along with a compelling and exotic stride to match her persona. She engaged readily with our weary group. Federica's passion came front and center as she coveted her desire to inspire us.

We awakened like wide-eyed and bushy-tailed squirrels on an unprecedented mission and rose to the five-star challenge.

"Welcome, my Tootie Frutti's. I know you are *very, very* tired. Jet lag, my Tootie Frutti's," Federica exclaimed with her warm, brown eyes scanning us on the bus. "But," she added with a slender index finger raised upward, a passionate voice, and twinkling eyes, "*each* of us is like a different fruit, no?"

Federica tossed back her exquisite hair of midnight beauty and laughed heartily. So did we, instantly caught up in her zeal. "*You* are an apple, *you* are a lemon…and, *you* are…" Federica continued, as her "signature" index finger pointed out different folks.

There was a pause. It was a purposeful pause accentuated with her perfectly arched eyebrow. "But, wait a minute!" she whispered, that mischievous smile creeping back across her exuberant face.

Then Federica spoke boldly. "You worry? You die! You don't worry? You die! *Don't worry,* be happy!" She threw back her head, laughed, and zoomed into a comical, diva pose with one hand on her hip and peered melodramatically at our group. What pizzaz and attitude! We hooted and applauded exuberantly with our outstanding and charming Queen Diva.

After another dramatic pause and a mischievous glance around our bus, the famous Federica grin came forth. All of us continued to watch her with childlike anticipation.

Federica's perfectly arched, black eyebrow made an obvious come back. "We take care of each other, no?" she inquired. Our heads bobbled like a bunch of little kids who adored listening and watching a creative storyteller. "I *always* take care of you, my Tootie Frutti's. *Don't worry!*" she exclaimed with her grandiose gestures.

Alas, no worries. With limited time and less desire for our computers and texting, we were relaxed. Instead, we readily became photo artisans as we traveled with joyous hearts and laughed until our bellies ached. We *still connected* supremely and made new friends.

We devoured Italy's divine array of seafood, fresh and delectable vegetables, and splendid fruits. And, of course, we happily drank sumptuous Limoncello and homemade vino (without sulfites!).

Our group trekked everywhere from the antiquity of "Magnifico Roma, Roma!" way down the intoxicating southern coast of Amalfi beauty. When we boarded a delightful ferry to ride across the Straits of Messina, Federica reminded us of the exotic journey awaiting us.

"My Tutti Fruttie's, we are *so* lucky. Not just Palermo, no? We explore the *three* legs of Sicily!" touted feisty Federica.

And, tango on, we did…

Our group continued to eat well, often, and with sublime pleasure. We ventured ecstatically to each outdoor market. We toasted and drank the nectar of the gods and goddesses. Federica adored watching us become enthralled with the southern countryside, Amalfi coastline, and the awe-inspiring "three-legs of Sicily" journey. Spot on!

No matter what happened (and, of course, things *did* happen), our group choose to adopt Federica's demeanor of splendor, ecstasy, celebration in the moment, and gratitude. We readily embraced her daily sentiment—"*No worries*, my Tootie Frutti's!"

The best gifts were on the horizon, yet to come into glorious fruition. They evolved in my divine dreamscapes and alluring discoveries throughout the journey in southern Italia and Sicily! My lifetime affirmations of inspiration, joy, laughter, and rejuvenating spirit came full circle.

I needed to share these memorable and best gifts in my book. And, of course, the grandiose epiphany that touched my mind, body, and spirit.

Tango on. Attitude = Altitude.

Dolphins at Play

Chapter One

Does Your Richter Scale Soar With Laughter and Play?

GRIN. WEAR IT TOO MUCH.

Beam upward… SPOCKASIZE!

Text yourself a hilarious message. Reply a-MUSE-ing-ly.

Smile until the edges meet your ears. Adore the sensation.

Big teeth. And, a lot of gum. Flaunt both!

Celebrate. Know that your play begets play.

Flaunt your "toe art" at a favorite beach. Be bodacious. Beam your "toe art" across a region, a state, or the world.

Be hooked by spring-fever mania. Go berserk. Let giggles arise from the deep abyss of the belly as you savor the surprises and enlightenments.

Be zany. Fill your tummy to the brim with stupendous, nonstop laughter. Silliness is free and fabulous.

Engage a stranger with an unexpected smile. You will make a difference in his or her daily journey. Let the abundance come full circle.

"Wicked good" playtime *always* stays in vogue. Go for it!

Multiple vitamins = a mega-dose of belly laughs per day. Overdose with the best and natural high in life.

Laughter, imagination, and play are a creative-smoothie delite. EnJOY!

A *talking* full moon is underrated artistry. Partake of the whimsical, mystical dialogues. Grin back at the moon like a Cheshire cat.

Why not today and *every* day? Let your laugh meter soar.

Peek-A-Boo Playtime

Now is An Opportune Time to Pause and Celebrate YOU! Reflect Upon Your Precious Moments of Laughter and Play:

Now is An Opportune Time to Pause and Embrace the Joys in Your Own Life! Reflect Upon the Mega-Boosts to Your Attitude and Altitude:

Sunset Moment

Chapter Two

Does Your Mind, Body, and Spirit Adore Joy and Rejuvenation?

BELIEVE YOU CAN AND YOU WILL EXPERIENCE LIFE'S splendor. Feel a new pulse resonate in your heart.

Radiate kindness. Watch others beam!

Pause. Greet the dawn and dusk of becoming.

Go to a drumming circle and meet your spirit. Yeha Noha…

Cock your head. Do you hear nature's whispers of love?

Release ego mania. Entrust intuition and the vibes of your heart.

Let silence become your soul's reprieve. Transcend the earthly pace.

Surf the day and flow in the moments. Rise above a time of darkness. Choose and pursue a resplendent light of being and becoming.

Open your heart to mystery, mystique, and miracles. Feel the transforming, inner peace.

Open your window. Let the mystical scents of evening drift into your dreams.

Splendid karma alters the quality of any journey. New beginnings await your quest to know. Open the doors and seize the essence of hope and abundance.

Your soul is serendipity, optimism, and self-love in the moment. Let the immersion begin.

Intimate connections are clasped hands and cuddling. Become a *soul*-mate.

Amazing grace arrives with the embrace of determination. Your verve is sustainable, renewable ener-chi.

Soul mates are joined at the hip and heart, Siamese twins in synchrony.

Soul mates

Now is An Opportune Time to Pause and Celebrate YOU! Reflect Upon Your Precious Moments of Joy and Rejuvenation:

Now is An Opportune Time to Pause and Embrace the Joys in Your Own Life! Reflect Upon the Mega-Boosts to Your Attitude and Altitude:

Enlightenment and Peace

Chapter Three

Does Your Ego Relinquish Ownership to Heartfelt Expressions?

Be *KOOL*. No worries. The attitude is contagious.

Let your "well of being" runneth over. Experience the gratitude.

Pay forward--a freebie hug. Feel the resonance…

Play the "no dinero" lotto of life. It pays dividends.

Do random acts of kindness. Remain anonymous.

Be still. Defuse. Release mind(less) chatter.

Bite your tongue. Rediscover the treasures found in silence.

Permit last year's follies to become a New Year's resilience. Rejuvenate!

Treat yourself with loving kindness…and others will follow suit.

Wade into a lake or ocean. Immerse into the mystique and beauty of your core being.

Thumbs up. Purposefully choose to create another day of livin' large.

The mountain summit is possible with verve. Accept and attune to your vibrant, courageous spirit.

Intentions of the heart can become stronger than your mind chatterbox.

Appreciate the calming connection of your mind, body, and spirit.

SPEED...Spirit provides *every* day, everywhere...divine! LIMIT...Love is manifest...is there!

U live, U love, U levitate. U evolve...

Starburst Heart

Now is An Opportune Time to Pause and Celebrate YOU! Reflect Upon Your Precious Moments of Heartfelt Expressions:

Now is An Opportune Time to Pause and Embrace the Joys in Your Own Life! Reflect Upon the Mega-Boosts to Your Attitude and Altitude:

Inspiration and Bliss

Chapter Four

Does Your Attitude Raise The Altitude?

BE SMUG…ABOUT LIVING LARGE. RAISE THE BAR. CREATE more room for smugness.

Let your spontaneity surrender to the unexpected joys. Surrender again…and again…and again.

Let any sorrow evolve into another lifetime lesson. Sat Nam ("I am").

Permit bliss to enter and re-enter your world. Cherish the full circle…

Be an inspirational, impassioned human being. Surrender to the evolution.

Share your talents and give plentifully. The art of reciprocal learning begins.

Wake up knowing the gift of another day. Honor the moments for gratitude 24/7.

Watch the sunrise. Let the sky art begin a day of enlightenments.

Watch the sunset. Let the sky art caress your soul.

Allow baby steps to count. Relinquish the urgency to know "how many" steps.

Know that determination can be visionary. Envision the vision.

To change is an act of bravado. Not to change manifests another intention and a different journey.

Making a choice *is* a choice. Pause...

Gratitude can become a daily practice. Patience, tolerance, humility, inspiration, and wisdom are no longer illusive.

The peaks and valleys of lifetime lessons influence the attitude. Self-love and forgiveness raise the altitude.

Gratitude for the Beauty

Now is an Opportune Time to Pause and Celebrate YOU! Reflect Upon Your Precious Moments of Unexpected Joy, Surrender, and Enlightenment:

Now is an Opportune Time to Pause and Embrace the Joys in Your Own Life! Reflect Upon the Mega-Boosts to Your Attitude and Altitude:

Harmony, Solace, and Rejuvenation

Chapter Five

Does Your "Tango On" Spirit Evolve Each Day?

SEEK AND DISCOVER THE QUIET SYNCHRONY OF "I AND Thou". Stillness and inner peace await your generosity. Savor this sanctuary of peace.

Transform the energy. Rebirth your mind, body, and soul.

Celebrate your *birth*day. Know and rediscover your *self*-worth.

Honor the arrival of a daily boost. The value and appreciation of your self esteem and dignity will be exponential.

Release the belly laughs. Levitate with your free spirit. Watch your zest for life become outrageously contagious.

Choose wisely. Become a guru or guruette.

Be attuned to your natural heart speak. Become the *real* deal.

The creme' de creme' is that you are you. Smashingly good!

Release the turmoil of any self-imposed hurdles. Inner strength manifests when you surrender and go with the flow.

Do not let overthinking run amuck. The ego can become a ravenous piranha, feeding upon your soul. Become a fearless, enterprising, and creative heart seeker.

In hindsight, the difficult times teach us to stretch. Human spandex!

Coming out of your darkness permits you to see the bona fide, radiant light. Inhale the breath of abundance. Exhale the impurities of dissonance.

You are a rebirthing soul that awaits authentic recognition and honorable choices. Own the bravado to choose attentively and faithfully.

Joy springs up when you trust going forward step by step. Offer your soul patience, loving kindness, and no judgements. Invite your "tango on" spirit to spring forth.

Your perfect imperfections illuminate the worthy passages along the journey. Let the splendor of your odyssey continue.

Free Spirit

Now is An Opportune Time to Pause and Celebrate YOU! Reflect Upon Your Precious Moments With the Daily "Tango On" Spirit:

Now is An Opportune Time to Pause and Embrace the Joys in Your Own Life! Reflect Upon the Mega-Boosts to Your Attitude and Altitude:

CPSIA information can be obtained at www.ICGtesting.com
Printed in the USA
BVOW07s0751061114

373879BV00001B/6/P